I0821234

Fables & Folktales

The Crow & the Pitcher

by Tyler Gieseke

Dash!
LEVELED READERS
An Imprint of Abdo Zoom • abdobooks.com

Level 1 – Beginning
Short and simple sentences with familiar words or patterns for children who are beginning to understand how letters and sounds go together.

Level 2 – Emerging
Longer words and sentences with more complex language patterns for readers who are practicing common words and letter sounds.

Level 3 – Transitional
More developed language and vocabulary for readers who are becoming more independent.

abdobooks.com

Published by Abdo Zoom, a division of ABDO, PO Box 398166, Minneapolis, Minnesota 55439.

Printed in the United States of America, North Mankato, Minnesota.
102025
012026

Photo Credits: ABDO, Artistly, Shutterstock
Production Contributors: Jennie Forsberg, Grace Hansen, Tyler Gieseke
Design Contributors: Candice Keimig, Neil Klinepier, Colleen McLaren

Library of Congress Control Number: 2025936788

Publisher's Cataloging in Publication Data

Names: Gieseke, Tyler, author.
Title: The crow & the pitcher / by Tyler Gieseke
Description: Minneapolis, Minnesota : Abdo Zoom, 2026 | Series: Fables & folktales | Includes online resources and index.
Identifiers: ISBN 9798384940036 (lib. bdg.) | ISBN 9798384940791 (ebook) | ISBN 9798384941170 (read-to-me ebook)
Subjects: LCSH: Crows--Juvenile literature. | Aesop's fables--Juvenile literature. | Pebbles--Juvenile literature. | Problem solving--Juvenile literature. | Perseverance (Ethics)--Juvenile literature. | Intellect of animals--Juvenile literature. | Fables--Juvenile literature.
Classification: DDC 398.2 [E]--dc23

Table of Contents

Fables & Folktales

Fables and folktales are both kinds of stories. Fables are usually short. They teach a clear **lesson**. They often include talking animals.

Folktales are **traditional** stories that come from a group of people. Adults often pass down these stories to children.

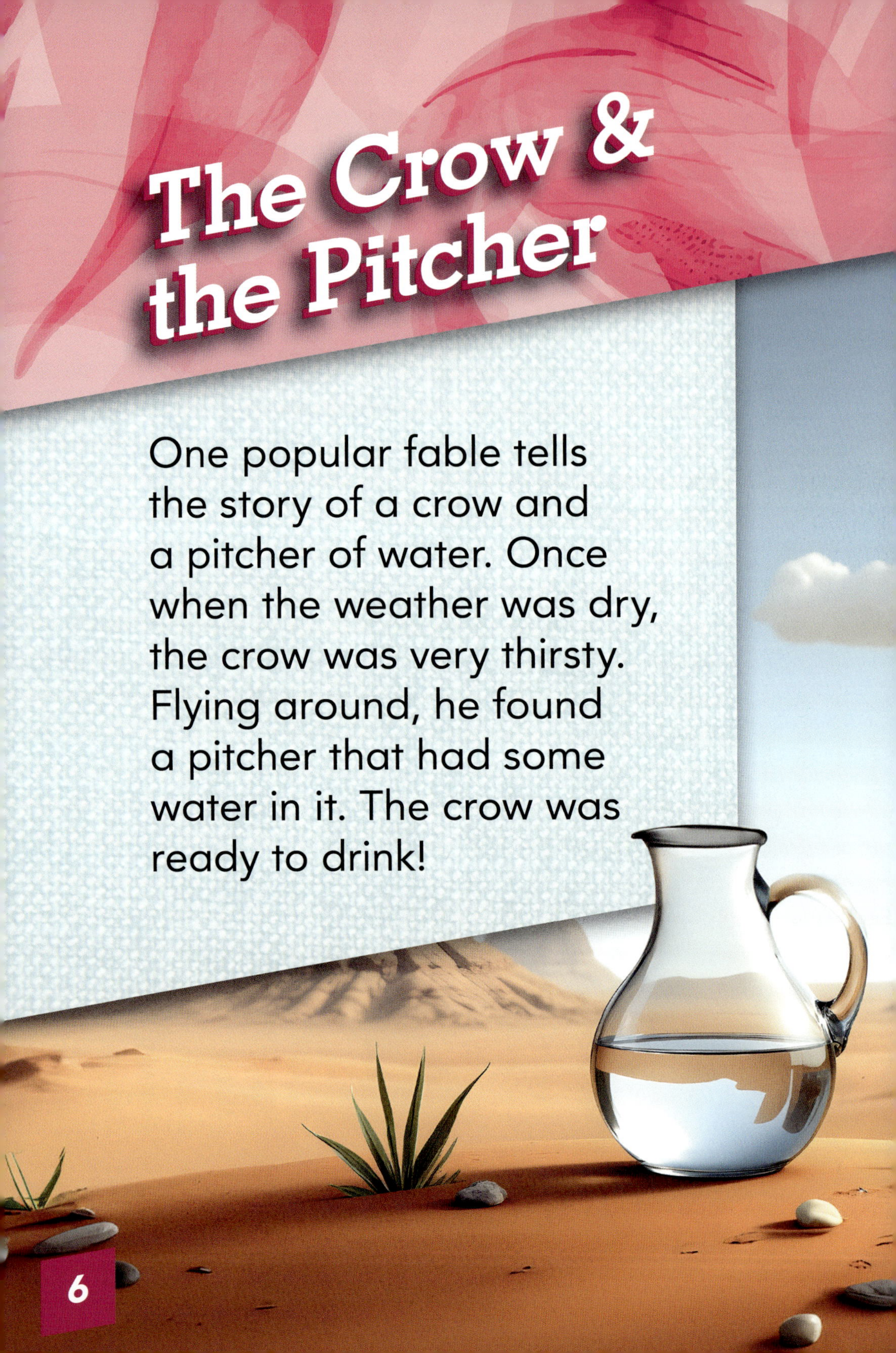

The Crow & the Pitcher

One popular fable tells the story of a crow and a pitcher of water. Once when the weather was dry, the crow was very thirsty. Flying around, he found a pitcher that had some water in it. The crow was ready to drink!

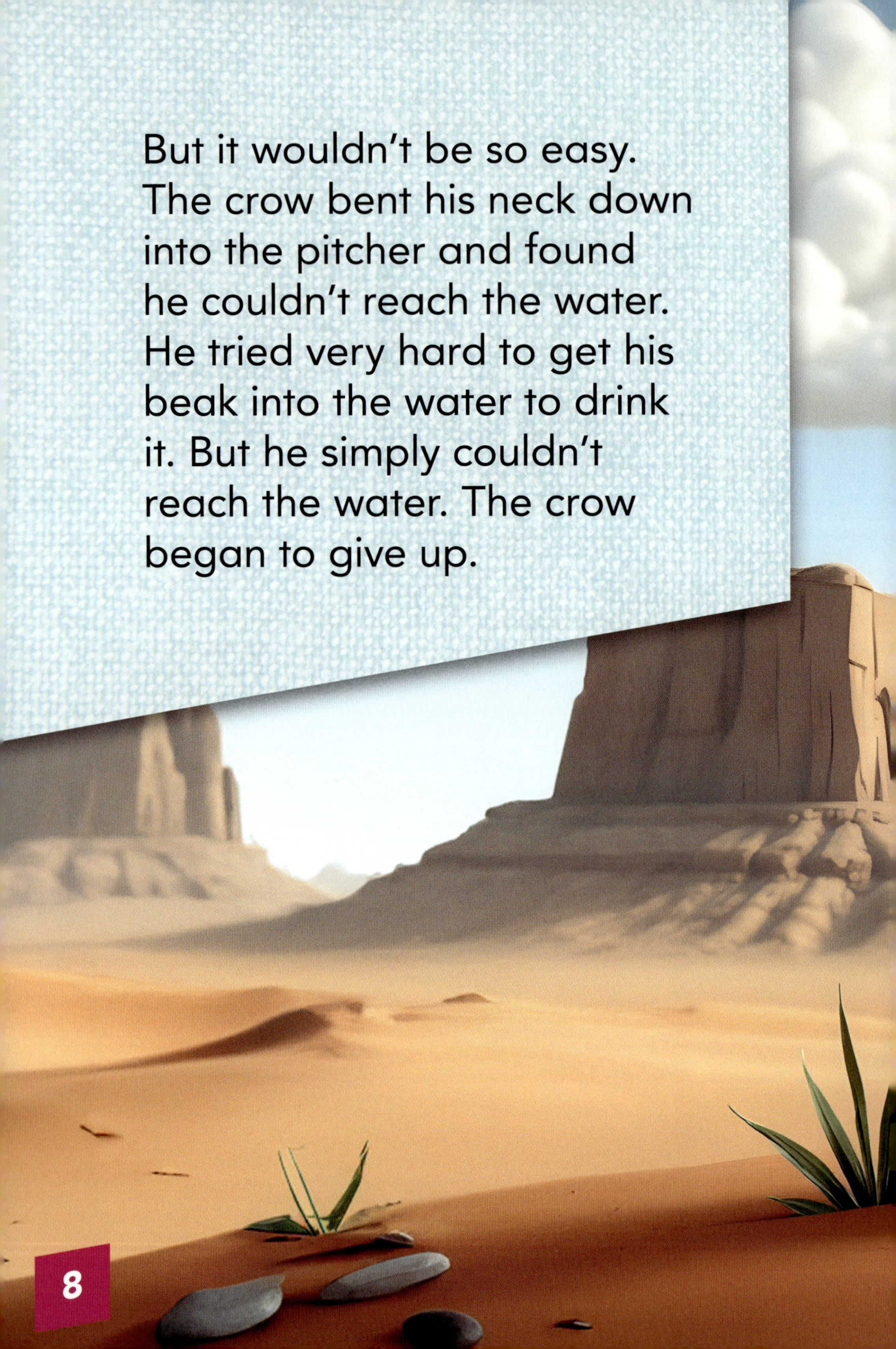

But it wouldn't be so easy. The crow bent his neck down into the pitcher and found he couldn't reach the water. He tried very hard to get his beak into the water to drink it. But he simply couldn't reach the water. The crow began to give up.

Before he did, however, he had an idea. There were some pebbles on the ground around the pitcher of water. The crow scooped up one of these pebbles with his beak and dropped it into the pitcher of water. Then he did so again, and again. One by one, the crow scooped up the nearby pebbles and dropped them into the pitcher of water.

Together, the pebbles pushed the water up to where the crow could reach it. Thankfully, the crow would not go thirsty. By using his wits and trying a new approach, he got around a problem. The crow thought he had learned something very important that day.

Lessons

The **moral** of the fable is that using our wits creatively can help us out of difficult problems. This is what the crow does in the fable. When he is **frustrated** and can't reach the water in the pitcher, he stops short of giving up. Instead, he thinks up a new idea. He uses the pebbles to raise the water.

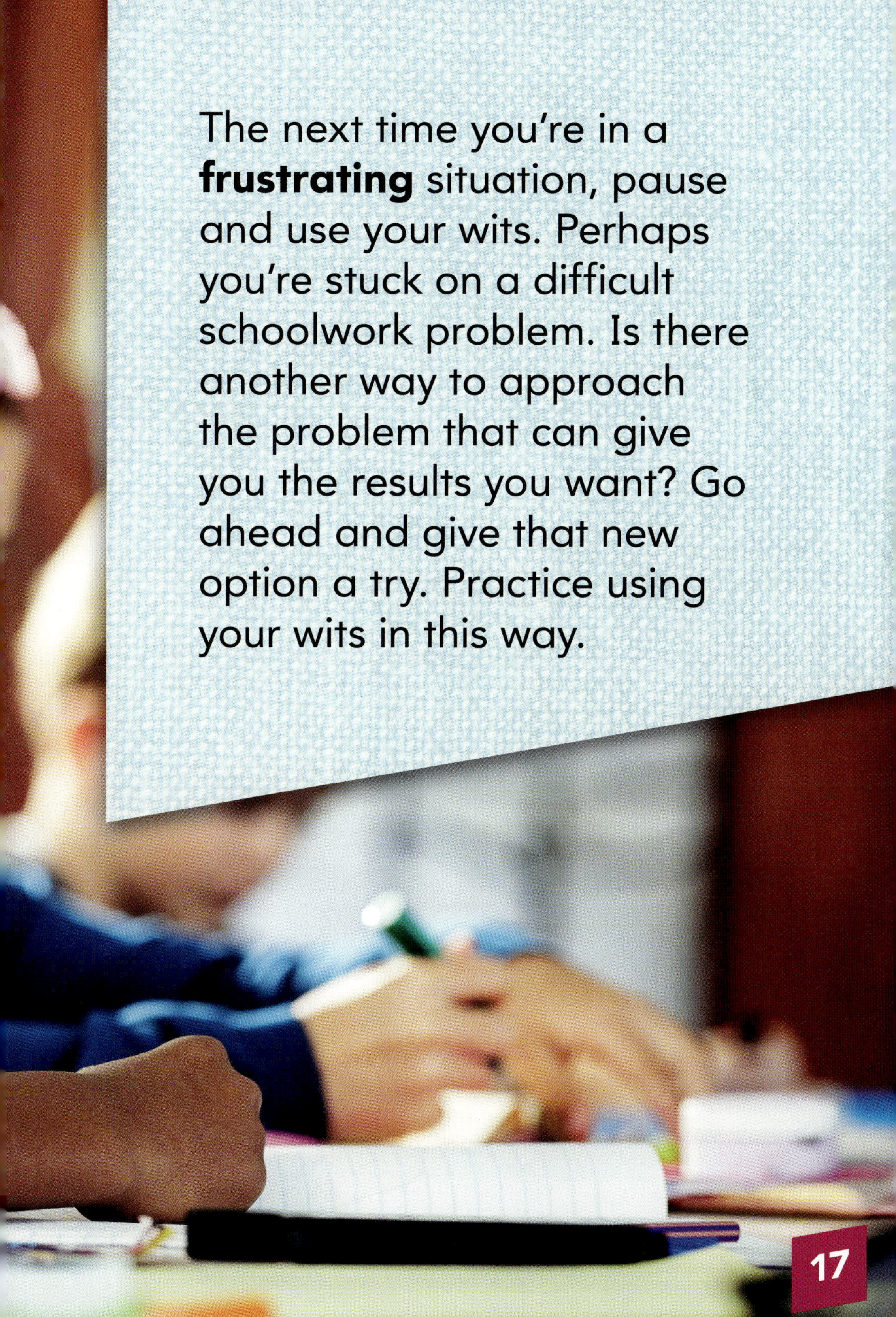

The next time you're in a **frustrating** situation, pause and use your wits. Perhaps you're stuck on a difficult schoolwork problem. Is there another way to approach the problem that can give you the results you want? Go ahead and give that new option a try. Practice using your wits in this way.

Another **lesson** from this fable is that there is more than one way of doing things. At first, the crow simply bends down into the pitcher to drink the water like normal. But that doesn't work. So the crow **invents** a new way of drinking water from a pitcher. The fable suggests that this is a good thing.

Remember that there is more than one way of doing something. You could try walking a different route to school one day to see how that **compares**. Or perhaps you could **invent** a new way of playing with a basketball or football! The possibilities are endless.

More Facts

- *The Crow & the Pitcher* is one of Aesop's fables. These are a famous collection of fables believed to have been written by Aesop.
- Aesop is believed to have been a slave from ancient Greece who later became free. He lived from about 620 to 564 BCE.
- But there are many different versions of Aesop's life and where he came from. Some people even believe Aesop never existed! They think he was made up.
- Like many of Aesop's fables, *The Crow & the Pitcher* has been retold over the years in stories and art.

Glossary

compare – to take note of the similarities and differences between things.

frustrated – feeling anger when you cannot reach a goal.

invent – to create something new and useful.

lesson – a teaching, or something learned.

moral – a teaching to take away from a story.

traditional – describing something done regularly and over time by a group of people.

Index

Online Resources

To learn more about *The Crow & the Pitcher*, please visit **abdobooklinks.com** or scan this QR code. These links are routinely monitored and updated to provide the most current information available.